D0409599

TOP 10 IN-LINE SKATERS

Jeff Savage

SPORTS TOP 10

Enslow Publishers, Inc.

44 Fadem Road	PO Box 38
Box 699	Aldershot
Springfield, NJ 07081	Hants GU12 6BP
USA	UK

http://www.enslow.com

Library of Congress Cataloging-in-Publication Data

Savage, Jeff.
     Top 10 in-line skaters / Jeff Savage.
        p. cm. — (Sports top 10)
     Includes bibliographical references (p. 46) and index.
     Summary: Profiles the lives and careers of Chris Edwards, Matt Mantz,
Fabiola da Silva, and other professional in-line skaters who perform aerial
flips, spins, and jumps.
     ISBN 0-7660-1129-1
     1. Roller skaters—Biography—Juvenile literature. 2. Roller skaters—Rating
of—Juvenile literature. 3. In-line skating—Juvenile literature. [1. Roller
skaters. 2. In-line skating.] I. Title. II. Series.
GV858.2.S38 1999
796.21'092'2—dc21
[B]   98-25724
                                                   CIP
                                                     AC

Printed in the United States of America

10 9 8 7 6 5 4 3 2 1

To Our Readers:
All Internet addresses in this book were active and appropriate when we
went to press. Any comments or suggestions can be sent by e-mail to
Comments@enslow.com or to the address on the back cover.

Illustration Credits: Maura J. Smith, Roces USA, Inc., p. 25; Photo by Brian
Konoske, pp. 18, 21; Photo by Darin Back, pp. 34, 37; Photo by Jeff Savage,
pp. 9, 13, 23, 41, 42, 45; Photo by Ken Greer, p. 15; Photo by Tony
Donaldson, p. 29; Photo by Voorhees, p. 17; Rollerblade Inc., pp. 10, 39;
Team Oxygen, pp. 7, 30, 33; Ultra Wheels, p. 26.

Cover Illustration: Photo by Darin Back

Cover Description: Matt Mantz

Interior Design: Richard Stalzer

CONTENTS

INTRODUCTION

TODAY, THERE ARE MORE THAN 20 MILLION in-line skaters. Most skate for fitness, fun, and to be with their friends. Others skate harder. They grind on rails, get big air, and do twists and flips off walls and launch ramps. They are the aggressive in-line skaters.

Professional aggressive in-line skaters travel around the United States and the world, competing in two disciplines—street and vert. In street competition, skaters zip around a course filled with ramps, rails, and box jumps. They perform a one-minute routine of jumps, grinds, and other tricks. In vert competition, skaters grind along the coping—the metal bar across the top of the ramp—of the U-shaped half-pipe and launch themselves high into the air in a fifty-second aerial display of spins and flips. In each competition (also called a comp), judges award points on style, difficulty, consistency, and form.

What do aggressive in-line skaters need to be great? First, they need courage. In-liners must have a total absence of fear. Second, they must be in top condition and able to withstand the pounding of hard falls. Third, they must have tremendous body control as they twist and contort themselves like acrobats. Fourth, they must be creative enough to choreograph a routine of exciting tricks. Finally, they must have the nerve to perform their routine in front of the lights, cameras, and cheering crowds.

Aggressive in-line skating started in the mid-1980s, around the time when a hot young skater named Chris Edwards jumped on a hand rail and grinded to the bottom of a staircase. Edwards and others demonstrated their tricks, but for several years aggressive, in-line skating remained a fringe sport. "Most people didn't understand us," Edwards says. "They just thought we were freaks."[1]

In the early 1990s, the sport began to catch on. By 1994, the first national skate tour was well under way as the National In-line Skate Series (NISS) staged several events in southern California. A year later NISS held nine events, many outside California. Also that year, the newly formed Aggressive Skaters Association (ASA) hosted three events, then twelve more in 1996. ESPN brought worldwide media attention to the sport in the summer of 1995 when it televised the first X Games (then called the Extreme Games).

With so many aggressive in-line skaters emerging in a sport that is still relatively new, it is almost impossible to pick ten skaters and say they are the best in the history of the sport. The ten we have selected certainly stand out, but there are others who would make someone's top ten list. Here is *our* list.

CAREER STATISTICS

Skater	Turned Pro	Discipline
MANUEL BILLIRIS	1994	vert
FABIOLA DA SILVA	1996	vert
CHRIS EDWARDS	1990	vert, street
ARLO EISENBERG	1990	vert, street
DAWN EVERETT	1995	street
KATE GENGO	1993	vert, street
TASHA HODGSON	1993	vert, street
MATT MANTZ	1993	street
ERIC SCHRIJN	1994	street
RANDY SPIZER	1995	street

MANUEL BILLIRIS

HE HAD HEARD THE REPORTS FROM TV NEWS: drugs, gangs, shootings. Manuel Billiris had heard about the dangers of America. Billiris's sponsor in Australia, Cozmo Wheels, was sending him to the United States to compete in the 1994 NISS competitions. Yet Billiris did not want to go. "When I landed in Los Angeles I was terrified," Billiris said. "I'd heard so much bad stuff about America. I thought, 'I'm going to get killed over here.' But I just learned to stay out of the dodgy places."[1]

The place where Billiris went was Spohn Ranch, a camp in southern California. There where pro skaters spent the summer working on their street and vert routines. "I walked into the place," he remembered, "and I saw Arlo [Eisenberg] just sitting there on a couch in the sun. I couldn't believe it. I was like, 'Oh, my god, it's Arlo! And there's Eitan Kramer! And there's Matt Mantz!' The whole house was crammed with international skaters. I couldn't believe I was there."[2]

Billiris had grown up in the small town of Darwin, on Australia's northern coast, where he lived with his mother, Terry, and his three brothers and two sisters. He played competitive youth soccer but grew to hate it and quit the game at age thirteen. His friends skateboarded, but he preferred roller skates, and remembers playing skating games at a local mall "with fifteen guys on skateboards," he said, "and me wearing roller skates."[3]

At age fourteen he packed up his roller skates and other belongings and moved two thousand miles to Melbourne on Australia's southernmost tip to live with his father, Charlie

Rising high above the earth, Manuel Billiris performs a trick on the half-pipe.

Billiris. "I'd never met him before," Billiris said. "He's a great guy. I wish I had known him sooner."[4]

When Manuel and his younger brother Menoli saw an in-line competition on TV, they decided to try it for themselves. They took the train into town, where they bought a cheap pair of in-line skates. "We tried them on at the train station on the way home," he said. "I skated up and down the platform. It felt weird."[5]

Manuel Billiris and his brother practiced on the hilly street in front of their house. One time Manuel got going too fast down the hill and couldn't stop. Just then a car backed into the street. To keep from crashing into the car, he purposely fell to the ground. That just made things worse. "I slid under the car," he said. "My foot got caught. The lady drove away dragging me. I pounded on the car, and finally she heard this pounding and stopped. I was all scratched and bruised. But at least I didn't break any bones."[6]

Billiris decided it was safer to learn at the vert ramps around town. He spent nine hours each day practicing tricks. Each month he aired one foot higher. After five months he was airing five feet. Soon he was on his way to the United States.

Billiris is known for his 720s (two complete spins in the air), but he's more than a one-trick skater, as his vert victories in three countries prove. "Skating is a mental thing," he said. "You learn the puzzle of your body. You have to figure it out. Solve it. It's a joy. I get tears in my eyes just thinking about it."[7]

BORN: September 25, 1975, Darwin, Australia.

HIGH SCHOOL: Sunshine Senior Campus, Melbourne, Australia.

HOMETOWN: Melbourne, Australia.

HEIGHT: 5 feet, 7 inches; WEIGHT: 150 pounds.

TOP FINISHES: **1995**: Extreme Games, Newport, Rhode Island, 3rd place vert; **1996**: World Championships, Lausanne, Switzerland, 1st place vert; Australian Titles, Melbourne, Australia, 1st place vert.

Although an injury forced him out of the 1997 X Games competition, Billiris remained in good spirits.

FABIOLA DA SILVA

Launching herself into the air, Fabiola da Silva shows why she is considered to be one of the best women's vert skaters.

FABIOLA DA SILVA

THE TOP PROS WERE GATHERED on the deck of the half-pipe in the sweltering summer heat of a Miami, Florida, afternoon. It was the 1996 ASA World Tour, and Chris Edwards was there. So were Randy "Roadhouse" Spizer, Eric Schrijn, Dawn Everett, and Kate Gengo. They stood together and watched as a new girl dropped in to start her routine.

She opened with a 360, then did another coming back. Next she did a series of soul grinds on the coping in which her front foot was perpendicular and her back foot parallel to the coping, sliding on the sole of the skate. The other pros watched in awe as she finished with an invert (a handstand on the coping) and a Miller Flip (a backflip with one hand on the coping).

Back on the deck, she hunched over, out of breath, as skaters came over to congratulate her. But who was this new trick master? Her name was Fabiola Oliveria Samoes da Silva. The other pros might not have been able to remember her whole name at first, but they knew she was good. So did the judges, who awarded her the first-place medal.

"It was my favorite moment of skating," da Silva said. "Everyone was coming up to me and telling me they liked me. They said, 'Oh, you're good. You are so good.' It made me feel good inside."[1]

Da Silva grew up in São Paulo, Brazil, with her mother, Claudette, her father, Ernesto, her younger sister, Fabiana, and her two dogs, Teka and Negra. Fabiola spent most of her time outdoors. She liked to swim and play volleyball, but by age twelve she yearned for a bigger athletic challenge. So she began kickboxing. Within a year she had become the Brazilian regional champion in her weight class. But at practice one day, an opponent broke her nose. Kickboxing was out. "I thought I better find another sport," she said.

In-line skating was in. Some teenage boys da Silva hung out with convinced her to go with them to a skate park. "It looked cool," she says, "so I started doing it."[2] She practiced hard and learned quickly.

Superstar Chris Edwards discovered da Silva at a local competition while he was on tour in Brazil. He convinced her to come to the United States to compete. She agreed, and soon became a member of the Rollerblade Riders (also called RB Riders).

Da Silva took first place in the vert competition in Miami, then won again at the NISS stop in Queens, New York. A year later, at the 1996 X Games in Newport, Rhode Island, she and her coach, Alex Aranah, were not notified that the women's practice time had been changed. She had only a few minutes to warm up before the women's preliminaries. It didn't matter. Da Silva performed crowd-pleasing backflips and was solid on the coping. She edged Jodie Tyler of Australia and Tasha Hodgson of New Zealand to win the vert title. Then, at 1997 X Games in San Diego, California, she won vert again to become a repeat champion. Aranah, her coach, said, "She is twice better than last year."[3]

Fabiola da Silva is widely considered the best women's vert skater today. "She's the one we all watch,"[4] says Kate Gengo. But da Silva is too modest to admit it. She is extremely uncomfortable talking about herself, saying, "I don't want people to think of me as a big head."[5]

FABIOLA DA SILVA

BORN: June 18, 1979, São Paulo, Brazil.

HIGH SCHOOL: Goaquin Leme Prado, São Paulo, Brazil.

HOMETOWN: São Paulo, Brazil.

HEIGHT: 5 feet, 3 inches; WEIGHT: 106 pounds.

TOP FINISHES: **1996**: World Championships, Lausanne, Switzerland, 1st place vert; NISS New York City, New York, 1st place vert; ASA Miami, Florida, 1st place vert; X Games, Newport, Rhode Island, 1st place vert; **1997**: Brazil Grand Prix International, 1st place vert; X Trials, Orlando, Florida, 1st place vert; X Games, San Diego, California, 1st place vert; World Championships, Sanctuary State Park, Florida, 1st place street; Seal Beach B3 Event, Seal Beach, California, 1st place street, 1st place vert; ASA Pro Tour, St. Jean Cap Ferat, France, 1st place vert; Overall ASA Ranking, 1st place vert; **1998**: X Trials, Virginia Beach, Virginia, 1st place vert; X Trials, St. Petersburg, Florida, 1st place vert, 2nd place street; X Games, San Diego, California, 1st place vert, 4th place street.

Fabiola da Silva was spotted by Chris Edwards while she was on tour in Brazil. Soon she became a member of Rollerblade's skating team, the Rollerblade Riders.

Internet Site (for more information about Fabiola da Silva):
http://www.rollerblade.com/skate/aggressive/bios/fabiola_int.html

CHRIS EDWARDS

WHEN CHRIS EDWARDS TOOK THIRD PLACE in both the vert and street categories at the 1996 X Games, he became the first male skater ever to medal in both disciplines at the same competition. It was just another first for Edwards. He won the first NISS competition ever held. He was the first ever to be sent on tour by a company. He was the first to have a skate named after him and the first to appear in a skate commercial. Next to Edwards's name there will always be the word *first*.

Chris Edwards' skating life began in Escondido, California, the summer before his eighth-grade year. He had taken a job at a bike shop. He was too young to be paid money, so the shop's owner, Martin Wizolski, paid him with points that he could trade in for goods. "There was this pair of in-line skates in the shop," says Edwards. "I thought they were cool, so I swapped my points for the skates."[1] Edwards rode his skates to football practice and to school, and he performed fancy tricks in the street. Other kids laughed at him. "They thought I was a dork," he said.[2]

One day the following summer, Martin Wizolski called Edwards into the bike shop, where a man was waiting to meet him. It was Pat Parnell, an employee at Rollerblade, Inc. "We want to hire you," Parnell told Edwards. "We will pay you to skate."[3] Edwards could hardly believe it. Rollerblade wanted to send him all over California, demonstrating in-line skates, for fifty dollars a day. Edwards agreed, and he began traveling.

Edwards had been an honor student with a grade point average of 3.6, but when school began in the fall, he

Chris Edwards is one of the pioneers of in-line skating. He has been skating professionally for over ten years.

dropped out. "I had to follow my heart," he said.[4] When he turned fifteen, the company doubled his salary to $100 a day. They doubled it again the next year to $200 a day. By 1992, he was making a $4,000 salary, plus $200 a day, and he was being sent across the country and overseas to Europe and Australia.

At the first NISS competition in Santa Monica, California, in 1994, Edwards took first place in both street and vert. It was the only time he ever swept the events. He could soar higher than anyone else, and he became known as The Airman. A few months later, Rollerblade introduced a skate named after Edwards. It was called the Tarmac CE (for Chris Edwards). Edwards received a royalty check that first year for $18,000. Then sales boomed. In 1995, Chris got $150,000. He moved to Minneapolis, Minnesota, to be near the company and help design two more skates, the Edwards Chocolate (street) and the Edwards Trooper (vert).

Today, Edwards is a millionaire. He owns a house on eleven acres, a boat, two Seadoos, four motorcycles, and all the skates he wants. He has appeared in commercials for Kellogg's, Kodak, HBO, Sunny Delight, and Coca-Cola and has acted as a stunt double in two *Mighty Ducks* movies. He still practices at least twenty hours a week and usually finishes high in competitions. "I've had my share of wins," Edwards says. "I'm stoked just to still be competing."[5]

CHRIS EDWARDS

BORN: December 22, 1973, Escondido, California.

HIGH SCHOOL: Escondido High School.

HOMETOWN: Minneapolis, Minnesota.

HEIGHT: 5 feet, 6 inches; WEIGHT: 160 pounds.

TOP FINISHES: **1994**: NISS Championships, Venice Beach, California, 1st place vert; **1996**: ASA South Padre Island, 1st place vert; X Games, Newport, Rhode Island, 3rd place street, 3rd place vert; **1997**: Ultimate In-Line Challenge, Orlando, Florida, 2nd place vert, 2nd place high jump; X Games, San Diego, California, 2nd place vert; Seal Beach, California, 2nd place vert; X Trials, Orlando, Florida, 1st place vert.

Edwards still competes at a high level and has displayed his talents in many movies and television commercials.

Internet Site (for more information about Chris Edwards): http://www.rollerblade.com/skate/aggressive/bios/edwards_int.html

ARLO EISENBERG

Sliding along the rail, Arlo Eisenberg is able to maintain his balance.

ARLO EISENBERG'S PARENTS were seated in the stands for the 1996 X Games street competition. They watched Eisenberg crouch in the starting area for his final run. Their son was locked in a battle with the sport's best—Matt Mantz, Chris Edwards, and Roadhouse Spizer—and they knew Eisenberg needed a stellar routine to win it.

Arlo Eisenberg had begged his parents not to come. "Please, Mom," he said, "please don't come watch me skate."[1] His parents, Vicki and Arthur, didn't listen. They came to Newport, Rhode Island, anyway. In the end, Arlo was glad they did.

"It was a big comp anyway, and then to have my parents there—I was afraid," Eisenberg says. "I'm glad they came, but it really made me nervous."[2]

Eisenberg opened with a 360 over the launch box, then chipped into a spine ramp and performed a breathtaking 540 (spin and a half) on it. Then, he hopped on a rail backward (backside grind) and did a royale in which he rode on the inside edge of his front skate and the outside edge of the trailing skate. Next, he did a half cab (switched from skating backward to forward), then a soul grind, then a royale. He capped his run with another 540 over the big box. The crowd roared, and Eisenberg's parents joined the cheers. Arlo Eisenberg had won the title.

Eisenberg grew up in Dallas, Texas, where he first tried in-line skating in high school when it was just a novelty. Soon his hockey skates and skateboard were in the closet to stay. "Rollerblading just seemed like the perfect marriage of the two sports," he said.[3]

Eisenberg traveled to southern California, where he and Chris Edwards were among the first competitors in the local comps. Soon he moved to Venice Beach to be near the in-line skating scene. After winning the 1994 NISS Street Championship, he became known as the King of the Street. He's been winning ever since.

Eisenberg's intelligence and creativity with tricks give him an edge over most skaters. He is not just an innovator with new moves, however. He also owns a company, called Senate, that produces skates and clothing products. His company also sponsors new skaters. "We get videos and calls from skaters all over who want us to sponsor them," he says.[4] An April 1997 *Newsweek* magazine article listed Eisenberg as one of the top 100 people to watch in the twenty-first century.

"I try to be a good representative for the sport, try to be as active in the sport as possible, whether I'm wearing my skates or not," said Eisenberg. "There's no telling where this sport is headed or how far it can go. The more we compete, the more popular it's getting. But I've always thought of it more as an art form than a sport. I'd like to think of myself as an artist."[5]

ARLO EISENBERG

BORN: September 7, 1973, Dallas, Texas.

HIGH SCHOOL: Arts Magnet High School, Dallas, Texas.

HOMETOWN: Venice Beach, California.

HEIGHT: 5 feet, 7 inches; WEIGHT: 160 pounds.

TOP FINISHES: **1994**: NISS Championships, Venice Beach, California, 1st place street; **1996**: Ultimate In-Line Challenge, Orlando, Florida, 2nd place vert; ASA San Francisco, California, 1st place vert; NISS New York City, 1st place vert; X Games, Newport, Rhode Island, 1st place street; **1997**: X Trials, Providence, Rhode Island, 4th place street.

Eisenberg, and his friend Brooke Howard-Smith started a clothing and skating supply company called Senate. Senate quickly became a multimillion dollar operation.

Internet Site (for more information about Arlo Eisenberg): http://espn.sportszone.com/xgames/summerx98/inline/bios/ eisenberg.html

DAWN EVERETT

As Dawn Everett Was Linking Tricks together on the street course at the 1997 X Games in San Diego, California, she was well aware that her final run had to be something special. With a few seconds left, she approached the launch box, and, with a blast of adrenaline, she jumped on the rail in a soul position. It was a good rail slide, but Everett wasn't finished with it. She reached down across her body in a twisted sort of way and grabbed her front foot. She was performing the ultimate grind—a cross grab fishbrain. And she was riding it clean, taking it down to the bottom. But an instant before she landed, her back foot slipped, and she fell.

The slip cost Everett a medal. She finished fourth. After her run she retreated under the stands to sit alone for a moment and gather her thoughts. She realized she had nothing to be disappointed about. She had gone all out. The trick was next to impossible to land, but she had tried it anyway. "What the heck," she said. "You can't win if you don't try the most extreme thing."[1]

Everett's aggressive approach to skating is no surprise when you consider her athletic childhood. Her mother, Shelley Everett, was her third-grade gym teacher and saw then that her daughter could be an athlete. "She had great coordination for her age, and she would play very hard," Shelley Everett said. "She certainly kept up with the boys."[2] Everett later played on a softball team that competed in regional tournaments, and she was the only girl on a local flag football team, playing any position the boys would let her play. "I was always a tomboy," Everett said. "I just

DAWN EVERETT

Dawn Everett takes a moment to rest during the 1997 X Games competition.

pushed myself to do whatever the guys did. The funny thing is, most of the guys I skated with growing up have quit skating."[3]

Everett grew up in Monterey, California, where she learned to skate on the recreation trails that wind through town, out to Fisherman's Wharf and Cannery Row, then along the Pacific Ocean. One time she was skating through an area that she did not know was off-limits, and a policeman gave her a ticket. She protested in court, and the judge agreed with her that the warning signs were posted too high. Her fine was waived. Another time she was cited for grinding on a bench along the recreation trail. This time she knew she was violating the law. The judge gave her two options: pay a $70 fine, or write a two-page paper on why she shouldn't skate recklessly. She wrote the paper.

At Monterey High School, Everett took honors courses and excelled at math. She enjoyed art class, and showed a special talent for drawing with pastels. Above all, she liked skating. In the spring of 1995 she entered her first competition, a local comp in Monterey—the Sea Otter Classic. She won the women's street division, which was easy since she was the only woman entered. In the fall of 1995, at an NISS comp in San Francisco, she jumped on a hand rail and thrilled the pros. "They all said 'Wow,'" Everett remembered. "That's what they said about me—'Wow.' They said they hadn't seen anyone better than me."[4] Everett turned pro, and she has been wowing fellow skaters and audiences ever since.

DAWN EVERETT

BORN: February 26, 1979, Monterey, California.

HIGH SCHOOL: Monterey High School, Monterey, California.

HOMETOWN: Monterey, California.

HEIGHT: 5 feet, 5 inches; WEIGHT: 120 pounds.

TOP FINISHES: **1995**: NISS Championship, Venice Beach, California, 1st place street; **1996**: ASA San Francisco, 1st place street; ASA Boulder, Colorado, 1st place street; ASA Chicago, Illinois, 1st place street; ASA Virginia Beach, Virginia, 1st place street.

Everett has always been very athletic. Aside from her professional skating career, she also competed in basketball and softball in high school.

Internet Site (for more information about Dawn Everett): http://www.inlineskater.com/profiles/dawn_everett.htm

KATE GENGO

Grinding down the rail, Kate Gengo hopes for a smooth landing.

KATE GENGO

IT WAS A MINOR COMPETITION. No world championship was at stake. No TV cameras were focused on the course. It was a small street comp in the summer of 1995 at a festival in San Diego, California. Still, Kate Gengo was going all out.

Gengo was about to perform a royale. She jumped toward the top of the rail but overshot it. She landed awkwardly on a down wedge and smacked onto the street—face first. Medical staff hurried over. Gengo looked up woozily at them, her face streaked with blood. "Do I need stitches?" she asked. Before they could answer, she jumped to her feet and took off skating again. "I spit out the blood and told the doctors to go away," she said.[1]

Gengo has a tiny scar on her cheek from that fall. That's nothing compared with the plate and seven screws in her left arm from a fall a year later in Miami, Florida. Gengo has suffered several breaks and bloody spills over the years, which makes sense since she has skated professionally longer than any other woman alive. "I've always been very physical," says Gengo, who will be competing at age thirty-six at the turn of the century. "I'm skating against girls half my age, so I need to think young and give it everything I've got."[2]

It's no surprise Gengo is a star performer. She grew up in an apartment complex next to the famous Lincoln Center in New York City. Her mother, Noreen, was a nightclub singer, and her father, Larry, was a professional tap dancer and agent for such singers as Tom Jones and Tony Orlando and Dawn. She and her older sister, Julie, and twin sister, Carrie, were given music and gymnastics lessons at an early age.

Gengo spent her summers near Toronto, Canada, where her grandparents owned an outdoor roller-skating rink. "I remember watching this girl roller skater who wore bell-bottom pants so long you couldn't see her skates," Gengo said. "She looked so cool. I wanted to be just like her."[3] Gengo learned to roller skate but didn't try in-line skating until a decade later.

In the meantime, she worked as a dancer at Walt Disney World, appeared in a commercial for Arby's, sang a voice-over for a Milky Way commercial, and acted as an extra in several dance movies, including *Fame*.

She was trying to learn in-line skating in New York's Central Park one summer day in 1989 when she saw a group of skaters jumping in the air and going down flights of steps. She followed the group down Seventy-second Street to a skate shop called Blades. Soon the skaters were teaching her tricks.

Four years later, Gengo and fellow pioneer Angie Walton were invited to a competition in Venice Beach, California. "It was Angie and me and a whole lot of guys," Gengo said. "Women's skating has come a long way since then."[4]

So has Kate Gengo. She writes articles for a number of skating magazines and helps promote the role of women in skating. She also works with children in her Brooklyn neighborhood and runs an after-school skating program. "A lot of people have helped me along the way," she said. "It's good to give help back where I can."[5]

KATE GENGO

BORN: January 27, 1964, New York City, New York.

HIGH SCHOOL: High School of Performing Arts, New York City.

HOMETOWN: New York City, New York.

HEIGHT: 5 feet, 4 inches; WEIGHT: 115 pounds.

TOP FINISHES: **1996**: ASA New York City, New York, 1st place street; ASA Vancouver, British Columbia, 1st place street; ASA Chicago, Illinois, 1st place street; NISS Miami, Florida, 2nd place vert, 3rd place street; ASA San Diego, California, 1st place street; World Championships, Lausanne, Switzerland, 4th place street.

One of the first women to become a professional skater, Gengo helps promote the sport to other women.

Internet Site (for more information about Kate Gengo):
http://www.xtremecentral.com/kategengo.htm

TASHA HODGSON

Inverted on the half-pipe, Tasha Hodgson hopes to score some points with the judges.

TASHA HODGSON HAD BEEN TRAINING with the top male skaters. Now it was time for her to show what she had learned. A huge crowd surrounded the half-pipe at historic Fort Adams in Newport, Rhode Island, for the 1995 Extreme Games (now called the X Games). Hodgson was new to the sport, and she was locked in a duel with long-time favorite Angie Walton.

Hodgson started with a 360 and a cab 360 (up the ramp backward), then did a stall, stopping on the coping in a soul position for a couple of seconds, then jumping off. She followed with an invert (doing a handstand with one hand while grabbing the skate with the other), then a Phillips 66 (a backward invert). With the crowd cheering wildly, she finished with an invert Miller Flip, and finally a forward flip.

Hodgson won the gold medal and raised women's skating to a new level. "The other pros respected me right away for winning," she says. "But winning wasn't important to me. It meant more for them to respect me as a person."[1]

Hodgson grew up on the South Pacific island of New Zealand, where she lived next to seal and albatross colonies. "I became an animal lover right away," she says.[2] At age seven she moved with her family to Auckland, New Zealand, and soon developed an interest in painting and playing the piano. She was not a sports enthusiast, but one day when she was in high school she went with friends to an old warehouse that had been converted to a skate park. The idea of skating appealed to her instantly. She bought a pair of in-line skates and returned the next day to the park to give it a go. She didn't know yet that the skates she bought were of poor quality and very slow. "I would drop in on the mini-ramp and wonder why I couldn't get up the other side," Hodgson said. "I thought I was really bad. I got so frustrated I almost gave up."[3]

Borrowing a friend's skates one day, she discovered the thrill of speed. From there, her skating career took off. At the 1993 New Zealand Nationals, she finished first in vert and second in street. The next year she went to Spohn Ranch, the in-line skaters' hangout in southern California. She lived there for three months, learning the tricks that would propel her to great heights. She became the first woman to do front and backflips at comps, and she established herself as the best female skater in the world at the 1995 World Championships in Lausanne, Switzerland. There, she won both the street and vert competitions.

Hodgson was the first woman to have a skate, made by Oxygen, named after her. With the royalties and other sponsorship money, she recently bought a three-bedroom house south of Auckland. She is among the all-time leaders—men or women—in victories, but she cares more about seeing the women's sport grow than about winning. "Skating to me is not about who's the best; it's about style and flow and making a run feel good," Hodgson said. "I just want to see the women's sport get a fair chance. They used to run the women's comp after the men's, and they would take down all the cameras and the audience would go home. I felt robbed. They weren't helping the sport grow. Now they're really starting to give women a chance."[4]

TASHA HODGSON

BORN: June 29, 1972, Otaki, New Zealand.

HIGH SCHOOL: Manurewa High School, Auckland, New Zealand.

HOMETOWN: Te Archa, New Zealand.

HEIGHT: 5 feet; WEIGHT: 100 pounds.

TOP FINISHES: **1995**: X Games, Newport, Rhode Island, 1st place vert; World Championships, Lausanne, Switzerland, 1st place street, 1st place vert; **1996**: X Games, Newport, Rhode Island, 3rd place vert; ASA San Francisco, California, 1st place vert; ASA South Padre Island, Texas, 1st place street, 1st place vert; **1997**: X Trials, Orlando, Florida, 2nd place street; X Trials, Providence, Rhode Island, 3rd place street, 2nd place vert; ASA Pro Tour, Dallas, Texas, 3rd place vert; ASA Pro Tour, St. Jean Cap Ferat, France, 2nd place vert; ASA Pro Tour, Milwaukee, Wisconsin, 3rd place street, 3rd place vert; **1998**: X Trials, St. Petersburg, Florida, 3rd place vert, 3rd place street; X Games, San Diego, California, 4th place vert.

Grinding along the coping, Hodgson plans her next move. Hodgson was the first woman to have a skate named after her.

Internet Site (for more information about Tasha Hodgson): http://espn.sportszone.com/xgames/summerx98/inline/bios/hodgson.html

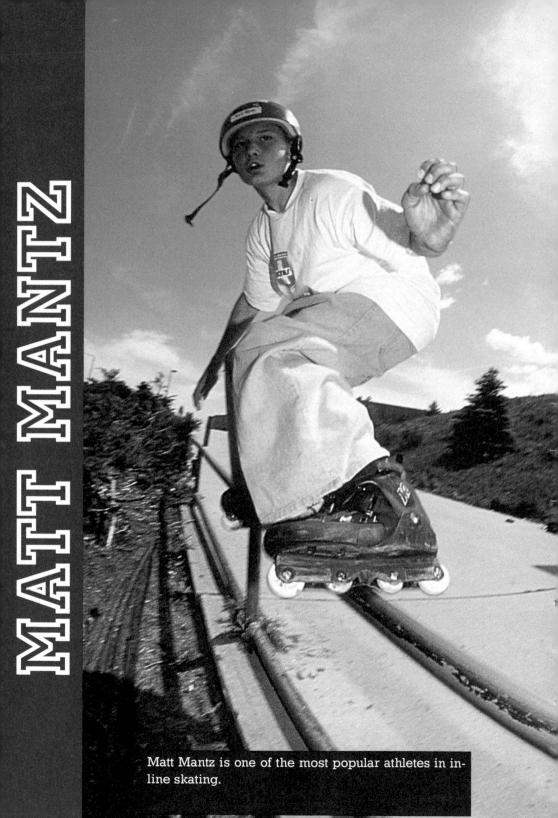

MATT MANTZ

Matt Mantz is one of the most popular athletes in in-line skating.

THERE WERE 160 SKATERS ENTERED in the street event, and Matt Mantz wondered whether he even had a chance. It was Mantz's first competition—a 1992 tryout in Huntington Beach, California, sponsored by NISS—and Mantz had come from Las Vegas, Nevada, to see how his skills compared with the southern California skaters. Mantz was just eleven years old and had been skating only a year, while most of the other skaters were older and more experienced. At four-feet five-inches and ninety pounds, Mantz was a small fry, and no one noticed him. But when it was over, and Mantz had won, he stood atop the winner's stand above the crowd.

Today, skaters and fans around the world know the name Matt Mantz. In a 1997 Internet poll he was voted Most Popular Skater. His house is flooded with fan mail. He even has a fan club. "He's like a mini rock star," says his father, Clark Mantz. "But when he's home he still has to take out the garbage."[1]

Matt Mantz grew up in Las Vegas with his four brothers and sisters, four dogs, four cats, and six goldfish. He showed natural coordination in youth soccer, and when he tried his sister Carey's skates one day, he wobbled around for a few moments and then was off down the street. Soon he had a pair of his own and went all around the town, wherever there were rails to grind or steps to jump.

Matt's father recognized his son's love for skating, so he built a course of ramps and jumps in the circular driveway featuring a launch ramp with a six-foot platform and a twenty-two-foot rail to the ground. Matt practiced tricks on the course and worked on his acrobatics on a huge trampoline in the side yard.

In 1994, when he began competing regularly, he was instantly identified by the other pros as a skilled young skater. Mantz still was small for his age, but he was able to get big air by using his speed and momentum. Since the 1995 Extreme Games he has gained eight inches and fifty pounds and has had to adjust his style. "The pants aren't quite as big anymore," he said, "so no one calls me 'Fatty Pants' or 'Little Big Man' anymore."[2]

Mantz has done stunt work for TV movies and owns a clothing line, called Hangers, that includes shoes, shirts, and baggy pants. As soon as he got his driver's license he bought a brand-new silver Mitsubishi Eclipse. He put 418 miles on it the first week. "I drove it in endless circles around the block for hours on end," he said.[3]

Mantz might be considered the most popular skater among fans of in-line skating, but around those who don't follow the aggressive skating scene, he prefers not to boast about his profession. "When people ask what I do," he says, "I just tell them that I rollerblade."[4]

MATT MANTZ

BORN: January 25, 1981, Las Vegas, Nevada.

HIGH SCHOOL: Clark High School, Las Vegas, Nevada.

HOMETOWN: Las Vegas, Nevada.

HEIGHT: 5 feet, 8 inches; WEIGHT: 138 pounds.

TOP FINISHES: **1994**: NISS overall, 2nd place street; **1996**: X Games, Newport, Rhode Island, 2nd place street; ASA New York City, New York, 1st place street; World Championships, Lausanne, Switzerland, 1st place street; **1997**: Ultimate In-Line Challenge, Orlando, Florida, 3rd place street.

Mantz makes this dangerous slide look easy.

Internet Site (for more information about Matt Mantz):
http://espn.sportszone.com/xgames/summerx97/inline/
97041athletes.html

Eric Schrijn

ERIC SCHRIJN WAS FIFTEEN HUNDRED MILES away from home, in the middle of his final run in a street competition, when he fell. He scrambled back to his feet, smiled, and finished his routine. Back on the start box afterward, he laughed and exchanged high-fives with pal Randy Spizer. Why was he laughing? Was he happy about falling?

It was the 1996 ASA South Padre Island comp at the southern tip of Texas on the Gulf of Mexico, and it was Schrijn's first major trip. Schrijn placed seventh, but he hardly noticed or cared. "I was just happy to be there," he said. "Everyone was competing and having a good time. I knew then that I always wanted to do this."[1]

Eric Schrijn (pronounced "Shrine") was a gifted athlete when he was growing up in Escondido, California, thirty miles north of San Diego. He played the popular sports—baseball, basketball, football—and was a standout defenseman in soccer. He was big for his age, lifted weights to get even bigger, and likely would have starred in high school sports had his mother not bought him a pair of in-line skates one Christmas.

Eric's father was shocked at the price of the skates. He guessed that Eric would try them for a week and then give up. His mother thought otherwise. "I unwrapped the box and saw these black-and-yellow boots with wheels on them," Schrijn said. "I was like, 'What are these?'" That day in 1991, Eric Schrijn put on the skates and rolled down the hill in front of his house. Naturally he had trouble keeping his balance. "I fell down a lot that day," he said. "So I just put them in the closet." His father was right—for a while.

ERIC SCHRIJN

Eric Schrijn is a very creative skater. He is known for his willingness to try anything during a competition.

"A couple of months later I got bored one day and decided to try them again," Schrijn said. "I tried harder this time. I still fell, but not as much. I stayed with it, and pretty soon I got the hang of it."[2]

Schrijn began practicing every day at a skate park in town. Slowly he improved. Chris Edwards noticed. Edwards lived in Escondido and was the idol of most skaters, including Schrijn. Edwards introduced Schrijn to the competitive side of the sport. Schrijn was eager to learn, and before he knew it he was a member of RB Riders, sponsored by Rollerblade.

At nearly two hundred pounds, Schrijn may be the biggest skater on tour. He is certainly among the most radical. Schrijn specializes in difficult tricks, which often cause him to fall and lose points with the judges. But he always gets up and tries them again. "Eric is not afraid to try anything," said Randy Spizer.[3]

"I don't have a routine," Schrijn said. "I do whatever trick comes to mind. I like trying wild tricks that I'm not sure I can even do until I do them. When I pull off something crazy, it's a rad feeling."[4]

ERIC SCHRIJN

BORN: December 27, 1979, Escondido, California.

HIGH SCHOOL: Orange Glen High School, Escondido, California.

HOMETOWN: Escondido, California.

HEIGHT: 5 feet, 9 inches; WEIGHT: 195 pounds.

TOP FINISHES: **1996**: X Games, Newport, Rhode Island, 3rd place best trick; Ultimate In-Line Challenge, Orlando, Florida, 2nd place best trick; ASA Miami, Florida, 3rd place street; ASA Vancouver, Canada, 3rd place street.

Skating in a street competition, Eric Schrijn charges toward the next ramp.

Internet Site (for more information about Eric Schrijn):
http://www.rollerblade.com/skate/aggressive/bios/schrijn_int.html

RANDY SPIZER

Randy "Roadhouse" Spizer patiently waits for his turn to compete at the 1997 X Games.

RANDY "ROADHOUSE" SPIZER HEARD HIS NAME called, and the butterflies in his stomach sprang to life. He was in Lausanne, Switzerland, in the final round of the 1996 World Championship street competition. It was hardly a time to be nervous, but Spizer knew that as soon as he was off the start box the butterflies would be gone. "It just takes a few seconds for them to go away," he said.[1]

Sure enough, once Spizer did his first trick—a 360 over the launch ramp—he was focused. He maxed out the course and himself, adding variations to tricks and aggressively working the rails. He passed T. J. Webber to take the silver medal, finishing behind only Matt Mantz. "It was my favorite performance," Spizer said. "Not because I finished second, but because it was so far away."[2]

Randy Spizer was born in Hensdale, Illinois, but he and his family moved to Moreno Valley, California, sixty miles east of Los Angeles, when he was two years old. His single athletic endeavor before aggressive skating was playing T-ball when he was five years old. "It was fun hitting the ball off the stand," said Spizer, "but my competitive baseball playing days are over."[3]

In the summer of 1994, Spizer was trying to figure out what he wanted for his fourteenth birthday when his friend Nick Leggatt suggested that he ask for rollerblades. Spizer asked his father. "OK," his father, David, agreed. "Let's find a cheap pair."[4] Randy started by skating out in front of his house. A month later he got a twenty-five dollar membership at the Moreno Valley Skate Park, also called Skate Underground. Three months later, he was doing tricks like the pros. Three months after that, he was competing against them.

Spizer is among the best trick masters in the sport and is known among in-liners simply as Roadhouse. He is part of the RB Riders team, and Rollerblade has produced a skate named after him. He excels at street comps with great balance, clean execution, and creativity. "He's a natural athlete," says Chris Edwards. "It's amazing how fast he picks up new things."[5]

"Skating is fun," Spizer said, "but I really enjoy being with my friends and being on tour." He even makes the most of his time now on those long airplane flights. "That's where I do a lot of my studying," says Spizer, who gets *A*s and *B*s. "School is really important, because skating won't be there my whole life."[6]

RANDY SPIZER

BORN: August 1, 1980, Hensdale, Illinois.

HIGH SCHOOL: Los Alamitos High School, Cypress, California.

HOMETOWN: Cypress, California.

HEIGHT: 5 feet, 4 inches; WEIGHT: 126 pounds.

TOP FINISHES: **1995**: NISS overall, 3rd place street; **1996**: World Championships, Lausanne, Switzerland, 2nd place street; ASA Chicago, Illinois, 1st place street; ASA San Francisco, California, 1st place street; **1997**: Ultimate In-Line Challenge, Orlando, Florida, 1st place best trick; World Championships, Naples, Florida, 1st place street; ASA Pro Tour, Dallas, Texas, 3rd place street; Overall ASA Ranking, 1st place street.

Spizer poses for a picture during a break in the competition. He ended 1997 as the Aggressive Skating Association's No. 1 ranked street skater.

Internet Site (for more information about Randy Spizer):
http://www.rollerblade.com/skate/aggressive/bios/
roadhouse_int.html

Chapter Notes

Introduction

 1. Author interview with Chris Edwards, June 24, 1997.

Manuel Billiris

 1. Author interview with Manuel Billiris, June 23, 1997.

 2. Ibid.

 3. Ibid.

 4. Ibid.

 5. Ibid.

 6. Ibid.

 7. Ibid.

Fabiola da Silva

 1. Author interview with Fabiola da Silva, June 24, 1997.

 2. Ibid.

 3. "Aggressive In-Line Skating Athletes: Fabiola da Silva," *ESPN SportsZone*, n.d., <http://espn.sportszone.com/xgames/summerx97/inline/970401 athletes.html> (August 19, 1998.)

 4. Author interview with Kate Gengo, June 24, 1997.

 5. *1997 ESPN X Games Media Guide.*

Chris Edwards

 1. Author interview with Chris Edwards, June 24, 1997.

 2. Ibid.

 3. Ibid.

 4. Ibid.

 5. Ibid.

Arlo Eisenberg

 1. Author interview with Arlo Eisenberg, June 24, 1997.

 2. Ibid.

 3. Ibid.

 4. *1997 ESPN X Games Media Guide.*

 5. Author interview with Arlo Eisenberg, June 24, 1997.

Dawn Everett

 1. Peter Madden, "Yabe lets skates do her talking," *ESPN SportsZone*, n.d., <http://espn.sportszone.com/xgames/summerx97/inline/ 970625womskate.html> (June 26, 1997).

2. Author interview with Dawn Everett, June 24, 1997.

3. Ibid.

4. Ibid.

Kate Gengo

1. Author interview with Kate Gengo, June 24, 1997.

2. Ibid.

3. Ibid.

4. Ibid.

5. Ibid.

Tasha Hodgson

1. Author interview with Tasha Hodgson, June 25, 1997.

2. Ibid.

3. Ibid.

4. Ibid.

Matt Mantz

1. Author interview with Matt Mantz, June 29, 1997.

2. *1997 ESPN X Games Media Guide.*

3. Ibid.

4. "Aggressive In-Line Skating Athletes: Matt Mantz," *ESPN SportsZone*, n.d., <http://espn.sportszone.com/xgames/summerx97/inline/970401 athletes.html> (August 19, 1998.)

Eric Schrijn

1. Author interview with Eric Schrijn, June 27, 1997.

2. Ibid.

3. Ibid.

4. Ibid.

Randy Spizer

1. Author interview with Randy Spizer, June 27, 1997.

2. Ibid.

3. Ibid.

4. Ibid.

5. Author interview with Randy Spizer, June 24, 1997.

6. Ibid., June 27, 1997.

Index